USBORNE SPOTTER'S STICKER BOOKS
INSECTS

Anthony Wootton

Edited by Rachael Bladon
Designed by Vicki Groombridge

Illustrated by
Phil Weare, Maggie Brand and Sue Testar

Cover design by Adam Constantine
Cover photograph by Claude Nuridsany and Marie Perennou/Science Photo Library
Series editor: Jane Chisholm

How to use this book

There are more than a hundred insect stickers in this book. Using the descriptions and the line drawings, try to match each sticker with the right insect. If you need help, there is a list at the back of the book that tells you which sticker goes with which insect. You can also use this book as a spotter's handbook to make a note of which insects you have seen.

Here are some of the words used to describe parts of an insect.

In this book you will find these signs:

♀ stands for a female

♂ stands for a male

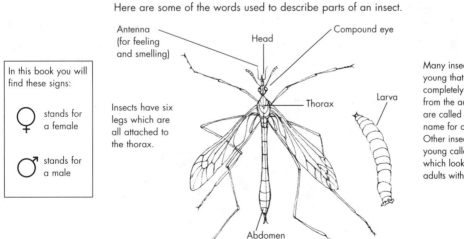

Antenna (for feeling and smelling)
Head
Compound eye
Thorax
Larva
Abdomen

Insects have six legs which are all attached to the thorax.

Many insects have young that look completely different from the adult. These are called larvae. (The name for one is larva.) Other insects have young called nymphs which look like small adults without wings.

Giant cranefly or daddy-long-legs

SCHOLASTIC INC.

New York Toronto London Auckland Sydney
Mexico City New Delhi Hong Kong Buenos Aires

BUTTERFLIES

Wall brown ▷

Place	Date

Wingspan: 44-46mm

This brown butterfly has spots that look like eyes on its front and back wings. It likes dry open spaces.

◁ **Marbled white**

Wingspan: 53-58mm

The marbled white has marbled black and white wings. It is found all over Europe, and is common in southern England.

Place	Date

Brown argus ▽

Wingspan: 28-30mm

This heathland butterfly has brown wings with orange marks near the edges. You may spot it in southern England, Wales and much of Europe. The males are said to smell of chocolate when they are courting.

Place	Date

Purple hairstreak

Place	Date	▽

Wingspan: 36-39mm

The purple hairstreak flies around the tops of oak trees. It has purplish blue streaks on its wings.

Clouded yellow ▷

Wingspan: 58-62mm

The clouded yellow has pale orange wings with dark edges. It flies here from southern Europe in the spring.

Place	Date

Brimstone ◁

Place	Date

Wingspan: 58-62mm

This large yellow butterfly is not found in Scotland, but is common in the rest of Britain. The female is pale greeny-white.

♂

Peacock ◁

Wingspan: 62-68mm

The adult peacock hibernates in the winter. Its large wings are red with brightly coloured eye-like markings.

Place	Date

Pearl-bordered fritillary ▷

Wingspan: 42-46mm

This butterfly has black markings on top of its orange-brown wings, and pearly spots underneath. It is rare and becoming rarer.

Place	Date

Small white ▽

Wingspan: 48-50mm

You might see this common white butterfly flitting around gardens, especially near cabbages. Its front wings have black tips.

Place	Date

Place	Date

Large tortoiseshell △

Wingspan: 62-66mm

This rare European butterfly has brightly patterned wings, which have blue half-moons along the edges.

MOTHS

Hummingbird hawk-moth

Wingspan: 45mm ▽

You might see this little moth hovering over flowers and beating its wings like a hummingbird. It has brown front wings and orange back wings.

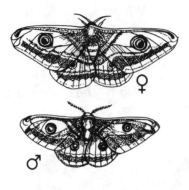

Place	Date

◁ **Emperor moth**

Wingspan: female 70mm
male 55mm

The male emperor moth has orange back wings, spots that look like eyes on each wing, and antennae that are like feathers. The female is bigger, with eye-like spots and a blue head. The emperor moth can be seen around moorland.

Place	Date

Lobster moth ▷

Wingspan: 65-70mm

The lobster moth is a dull grey-brown colour. It takes its name from the larva's tail end, which looks like a lobster's claw.

Place	Date

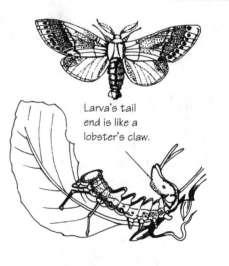

Larva's tail end is like a lobster's claw.

Peach blossom ▽

Wingspan: 35mm

The peach blossom can be found in woodland. It takes its name from the pink spots on its brown front wings.

Place	Date

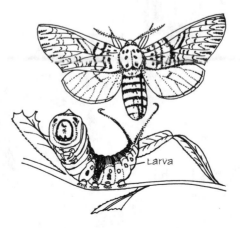

Larva

Puss moth

◁ Wingspan: 65-80mm

The puss moth is pale pink and grey, and is common throughout Britain. When its larva is alarmed, thin red "whips" stick out of its tails.

Place	Date

Clifden nonpareil or blue underwing ▷

Place	Date

Wingspan: 90mm

This moth is very rare, but you might come across it in eastern or southern England. It has mottled grey front wings and dark back wings with pale blue stripes around them.

Red underwing ▽

Wingspan: 80mm

This moth flashes its red and black back wings when it is threatened by birds. The colour of its front wings matches the bark of trees.

Place	Date

◁ Vapourer

Wingspan: 35mm

The male vapourer has brown wings, but the female only has wing stubs and cannot fly. The vapourer can be found all over Britain.

Place	Date

Larva

Oak eggar ▽

Wingspan: 50-65mm

The oak eggar has brown wings, with yellow edges and a white spot on each front wing. The male's antennae are like feathers.

Place	Date

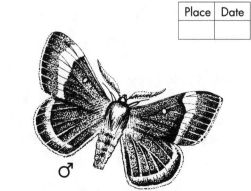

Silver Y △

Wingspan: 40mm

The silver Y is a dull-coloured moth, with white markings on its front wings shaped like the letter "Y". It flies by day and can often be seen in late summer taking nectar from flowers.

Place	Date

5

MOTHS

Lappet ▷

Wingspan: 60-70mm

Place	Date

The lappet holds its veined brown wings so that they overlap, making it look like a bunch of leaves. Its larva has black lumps called "lappets" sticking out of its head.

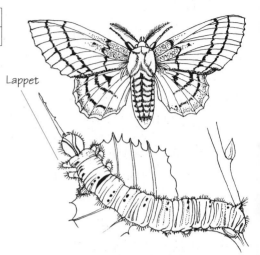

Lappet

△

Wood tiger

Wingspan: 35-40mm

You might spot this rare brown and cream patterned moth in open woodland and on hillsides and heaths.

Place	Date

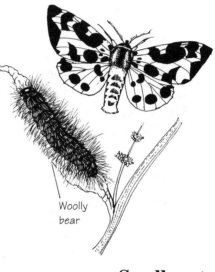

Woolly bear

◁ ## Garden tiger

Wingspan: 60-70mm

The garden tiger has orange back wings with black spots on them. Its front wings are mottled brown and cream. This moth's larva is called "woolly bear".

Place	Date

Swallow-tailed moth ▽

Wingspan: 56mm

This pale-coloured moth has large petal-shaped wings which make it look like a butterfly. It flies in a weak, fluttering way.

Place	Date

♂

Ghost moth △

Wingspan: 50-60mm

Place	Date

The female ghost moth's wings are browner than the white male's, and it is therefore better camouflaged. This moth is not often seen, even though it is extremely common.

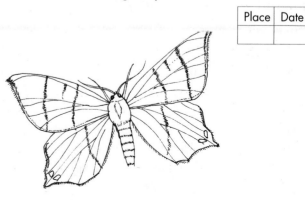

Cinnabar ▷

Wingspan: 40-45mm

You might see this moth flying short distances by day. It has red back wings and its brown front wings are marked with two spots and two red streaks. Its yellow and black larva can be seen on ragwort.

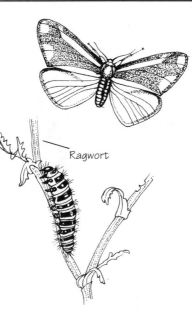

Ragwort

Place	Date

Six-spot burnet ▽

Wingspan: 35mm

The six-spot burnet takes its name from the six red spots it has on each brown front wing. Its back wings are red, and its bright colour warns birds that it tastes bad.

Place	Date

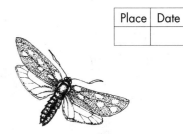

Markings like a human skull

◁ # Death's head hawk-moth

Place	Date

Wingspan: 100-125mm

This rare moth is named after the markings on its thorax, which look like a human skull. Its front wings are patterned brown and its back wings are light brown with darker stripes. The death's head hawk-moth lays its eggs on potato leaves.

Forester ▷

Wingspan: 25-27mm

This rare little moth has green front wings and pale back wings. It may be seen flying over meadows and heathland in the summer.

Place	Date

▽ # Eyed hawk-moth

Wingspan: 75-80mm

The eyed hawk-moth has large eye-like markings on its pink and brown back wings. It flashes these to frighten off its enemies.

Place	Date

BEETLES

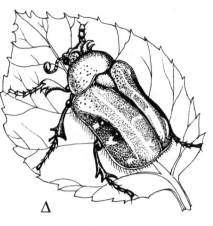

△

Musk beetle ▷
Length: 20-32mm

This beetle has a very long green body and even longer beady antennae.

Place	Date

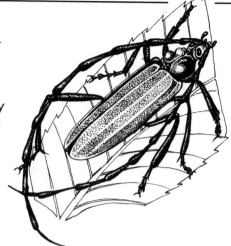

Rose chafer
Length: 14-20mm

The green rose chafer's wing cases are almost square in shape, but the front of its thorax is very round. It is mainly to be found in southern Britain.

Place	Date

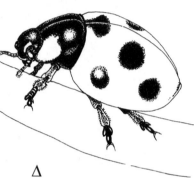

△

Seven-spot ladybird
Length: 6-7mm

The red ladybird, with its seven black spots, is very common in Britain. It can be seen on sunny days.

Place	Date

Cockchafer or maybug
Length: 25-30mm   ▽

You might see this beetle flying up to lit windows in the early summer. It has brown wing cases and a black head with fur underneath its thorax.

Place	Date

▽ **Water beetle**
Length: 7-8mm

Water beetles are very common, and vary in colour from brown to black. This one has a brown body with black markings on its wing cases.

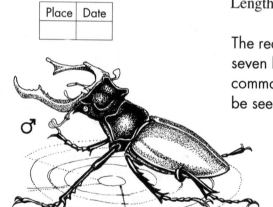

△

Stag beetle
Length: 25-75mm

Place	Date

The stag beetle is the largest beetle in Britain. The male has purplish wing cases, a black head and legs, and long antlers.

Great diving beetle ▷

Length: 30-35mm

You might find the great diving beetle in lakes and ponds. Its body is black with light brown edges, and it has brown legs and antennae.

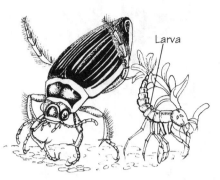

Larva

Place	Date

Place	Date

Cardinal beetle

Length: 15-17mm

There are different kinds of cardinal beetle. This one has a long red body, and antennae with branches all along them. It can be found on flowers and under bark.

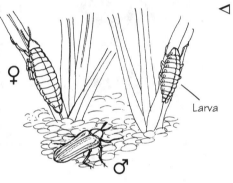

♀

Larva

♂

◁ **Glow-worm**

Male length: 15mm
Female length: 20mm

The female glow-worm has a long brown body with no wings or wing-cases. She attracts the male with her glowing tail.

Place	Date

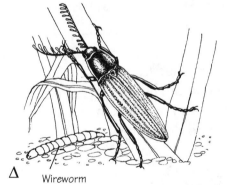

△ Wireworm

Click beetle or skip-jack

Length: 14-18mm

Place	Date

This rare click beetle has a sleek green body, with small branches all along its antennae. Its larva is called "wireworm".

Red and black burying beetle ▷

Length: 15-20mm

This beetle has two large red streaks across its black wing cases. It feeds on dead animals, biting their flesh and then burying their bodies.

Place	Date

BEETLES

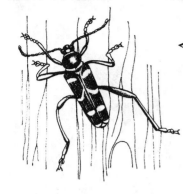

Wasp beetle

Place	Date

Length: 15mm

This beetle looks like a wasp, with yellow stripes along its brown body. It flies around flowers on sunny days.

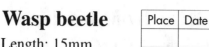

Place	Date

Colorado beetle ▷

Length: 10-12mm

You should tell the police if you spot one of these beetles, which damage potato crops. You can recognize a colorado beetle by its rounded body and the dark and light brown stripes along its wing cases.

Larva

Place	Date

△

Bloody-nosed beetle

Length: 10-20mm

When this beetle is threatened, it shoots a bright red fluid from its mouth. The bloody-nosed beetle has round black wing cases and a rectangular black section behind its head.

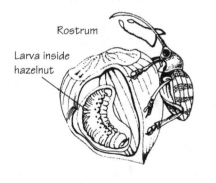

Rostrum

Larva inside hazelnut

Green tortoise beetle ▽

Place	Date

Length: 6-8mm

This green beetle has a rounded body and, when its legs and antennae are hidden, it looks like a tortoise. Its larva has a fork in its tail for holding skins and droppings.

Nut weevil △

Place	Date

Length: 10mm

The female nut weevil has a very long snout and a rounded brown body. She uses her snout (called a "rostrum") to make holes in young hazelnuts, where she lays her single egg. The larva then grows inside the nut, eating the kernel.

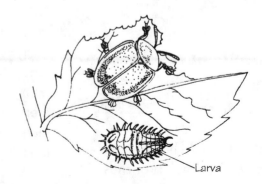

Larva

Devil's coach horse or cocktail beetle ▷

Place	Date

Length: 25-30mm

This black beetle can often be found in gardens. It has a long abdomen, which can release a poisonous liquid.

Larva

◁ ## Horned dung beetle or minotaur beetle

Place	Date

Length: 12-18mm

This black beetle has broad ribbed wing cases, thick horny legs and large horns around its head.

Great silver water beetle

Place	Date

Length: 37-48mm ▽

This is the largest water beetle in Britain, though you would be very lucky to see it. It has a large black body, with hairy back legs and claws on its front legs.

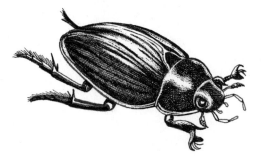

Death watch beetle △

Place	Date

Length: 7-10mm

The noise this beetle makes, knocking its head on the walls of the tunnels it builds, was once thought to mean that someone was about to die. The death watch beetle is mottled dark and light brown. It eats the wood in barns and old damp timber buildings.

Rove beetle ▷

Place	Date

Length: 20mm

There are different kinds of rove beetle. This one has red eyes and legs, a red section in the thorax and a long black tail. Rove beetles eat dead animals and birds.

BUGS

Water boatman or backswimmer

▷

Place	Date

Length: 15mm

The water boatman's brown body is rather like a little boat. It swims on its back, with the tips of its legs clinging to the underside of the water surface. Its back legs are shaped like paddles and fringed with hairs. The water boatman can be found in pools, canals, ditches and water tanks, but if its home dries up it can fly away.

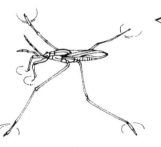

◁ ## Pond skater

Place	Date

Length: 8-10mm

Pond skaters are small, with very long legs and thin bodies. Their front legs are specially shaped to catch dead or dying insects that fall on the water surface.

Saucer bug ▽

Length: 12-16mm

The saucer bug is so-called because of the shape of its body. It has short legs, and the front ones are rounded and very sharp. The saucer bug can stab you with its jaws.

Place	Date

Water cricket ▷

Length: 6-7mm

The water cricket has long legs, and a dark body with two light brown stripes along it. You can find it on the surface of still water, eating insects and spiders.

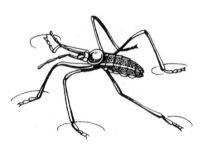

Place	Date

Black and red froghopper ▷

Length: 9-10mm

This red and black striped bug jumps when it is disturbed. Most froghopper nymphs produce froth.

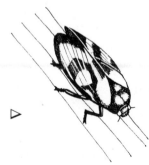

Place	Date

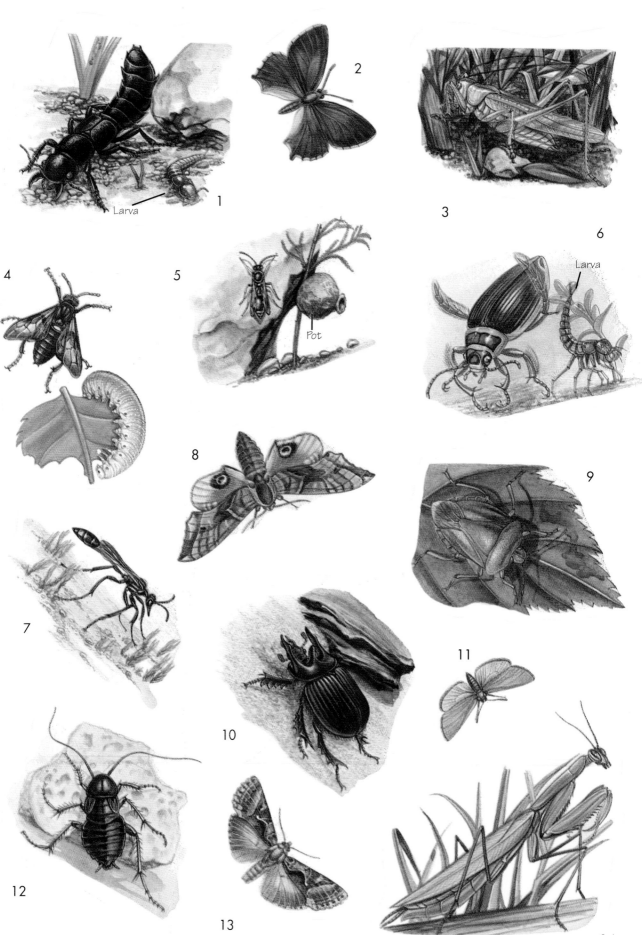

Larva

1

2

3

4

5

Pot

6

Larva

7

8

9

10

11

12

13

14

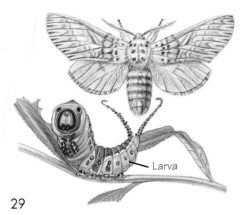

29

Larva

30

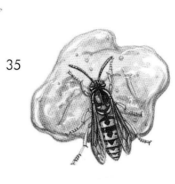

♂

♀

31

32

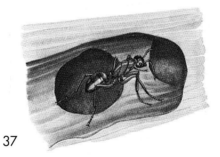

35

33

34

36

37

38

39

40

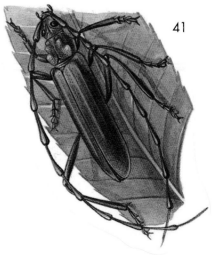

41

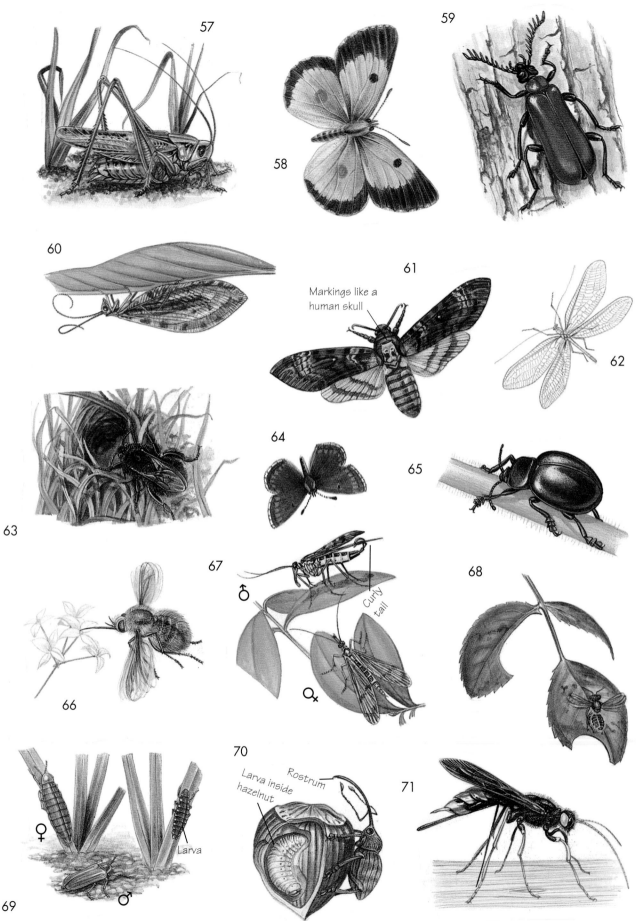

57

58

59

60

61
Markings like a
human skull

62

63

64

65

66

67
♂
♀
Curly
tail

68

69
♀
♂
Larva

70
Larva inside
hazelnut
Rostrum

71

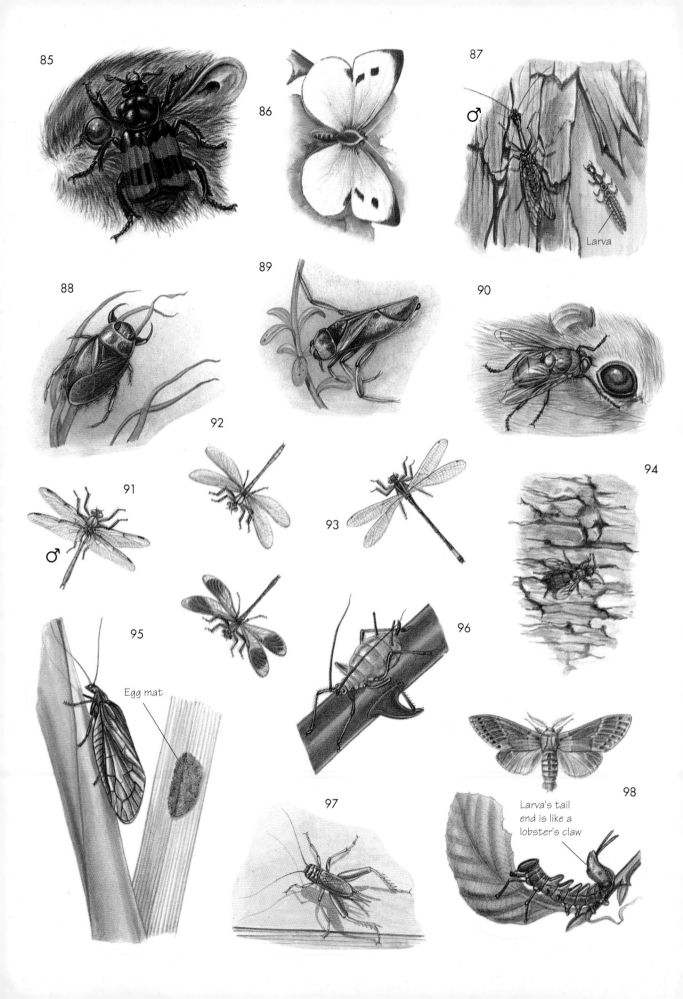

85

86

87 ♂ Larva

88

89

90

91 ♂

92

93

94

95 Egg mat

96

97

98 Larva's tail end is like a lobster's claw

99

100

101

Ragwort

102

103

Woolly bear

104

Ovipositor

105

Larva

106

107

110

Larva

108

Larva in hollow

109

♂

111

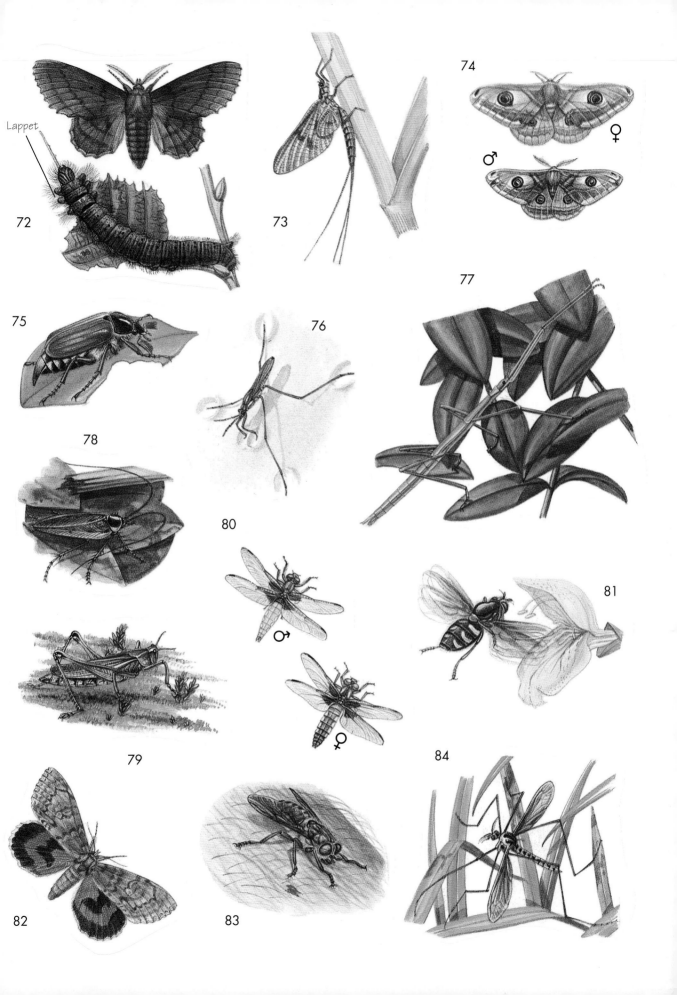

72

Lappet

73

74

♀

♂

75

76

77

78

80

♂

♀

81

79

82

83

84

42

43

44

45

46

47

48

49

50

51

52

53

54 ♀

55

56 Breathing tube

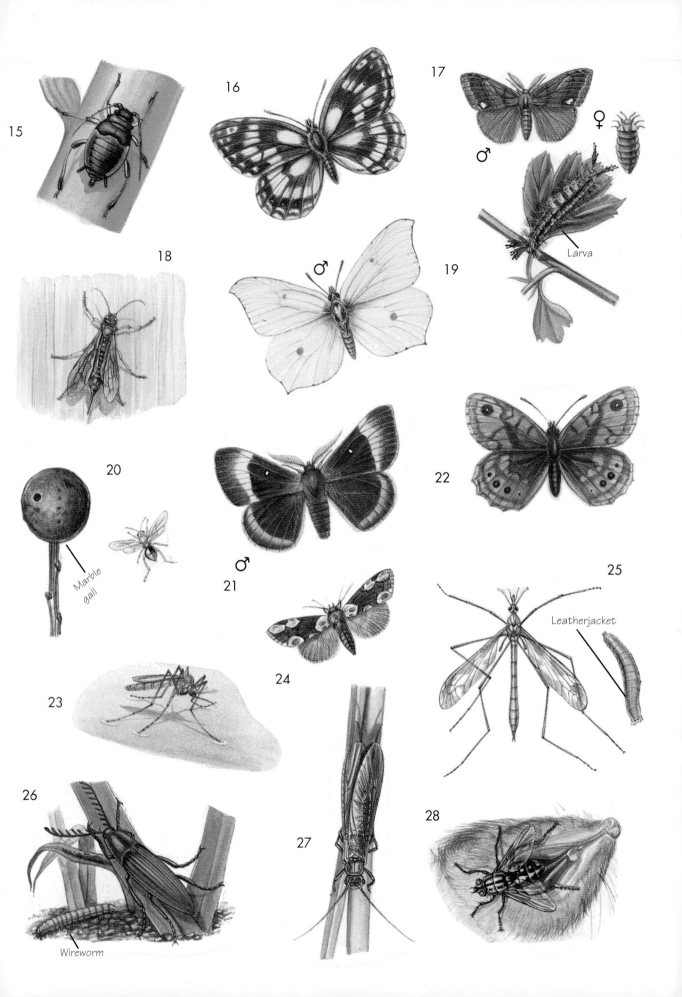

15

16

17

♀

♂

Larva

18

19

♂

20

Marble
gall

21

♂

22

23

24

25

Leatherjacket

26

27

28

Wireworm

Green shieldbug

Place	Date

▷

Length: 12-14mm

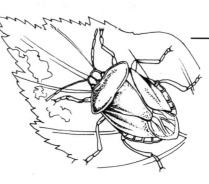

You might find the green shieldbug on trees like hazel and birch. It has a broad green body, with a light brown abdomen and beady antennae.

◁ ## Green leafhopper

Length: 6-9mm

This bug has a long straight green body with brown legs. It is common all over Britain, and feeds on grasses and rushes.

Place	Date

Black bean aphid or blackfly

Length: 2-3mm ▽

You might find colonies of this tiny bug on broad beans or thistles. The black bean aphid has a rounded black body.

Place	Date

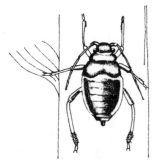

Rose aphid or greenfly ▷

Length: 2-3mm

The rose aphid, or greenfly, is shaped like a bulb, and can be green or pinkish. Its antennae are long compared to its body. This bug feeds on roses in the spring, making itself a pest. It produces honeydew, which ants eat.

Place	Date

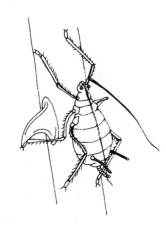

Water scorpion ▷

Length: 18-22mm

The water scorpion has claw-like front legs which it uses to catch small fishes, tadpoles and insect larvae. It has a brown body with a long breathing tube sticking out behind.

Place	Date

Breathing tube

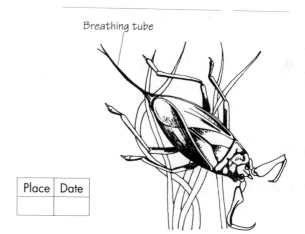

Dragonflies, Damselflies

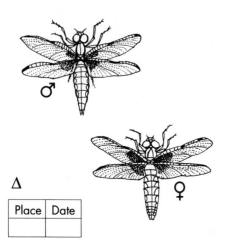

△

Place	Date

Broad-bodied chaser or broad-bodied libellula

Wingspan: 75mm

This dragonfly is common in southern England. The male is a pale blue with yellow markings, and the female is yellow.

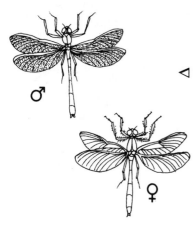

Ruddy darter or ruddy sympetrum   ▷

Wingspan: 55mm

You can find this insect around weedy ponds or ditches in marshy areas. It is golden-brown with transparent wings.

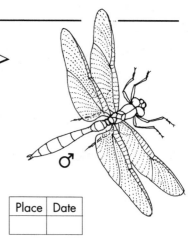

Place	Date

◁ **Downy emerald**

Wingspan: 68mm

This dragonfly has a bright green body and transparent wings. It can only be found in certain areas, but in these it is common.

Place	Date

◁ **Demoiselle agrion or beautiful demoiselle**

Wingspan: 58-63mm

The demoiselle agrion has a green body and wings with long thick veins, which are brown on the female.

Place	Date

Place	Date

Common ischnura or blue-tailed damselfly

Wingspan: 35mm   ▷

This dragonfly has transparent wings, and a blue tip on its long body. It can be found resting on plants in wet areas.

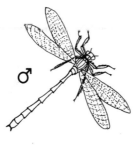

Place	Date

Banded agrion △   ♀ or banded demoiselle

Wingspan: 60-65mm

The male is blue with bright blue flashes on its wings, while the female is green with transparent green wings. This insect is rare in northern England and has not been recorded in Scotland.

BEES, WASPS

Red-tailed bumblebee ▷

Place	Date

Length: 22mm

This bee has a big black furry body with an orange-red tip. It is common in gardens. The queen makes her nest in a hole in the ground.

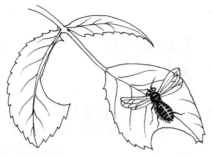

Potter wasp ▷

Place	Date

Male length: 12mm
Female length: 14mm

This very rare wasp makes small clay pots for its larvae. It then fills the pots with little caterpillars which it paralyses with its sting. This potter wasp has black and yellow stripes on the tip of its abdomen.

Ruby-tailed wasp ▷

Place	Date

Length: 12mm

This wasp takes its name from its bright red abdomen, but it is also known as a "cuckoo-wasp". This is because the female lays her egg in the nest of another bee or wasp. The larva then eats the food, egg or larva of that bee or wasp.

◁ Leaf-cutter bee

Place	Date

Male length: 10mm
Female length: 11mm

The leaf-cutter bee cuts semi-circular pieces from rose leaves to make cylinders where the female lays a single egg. It stores these cylinders in hollow stems and dead wood. This leaf-cutter bee is small and green.

Pot

◁ Sand wasp

Place	Date

Length: 28-30mm

The sand wasp digs in the sand and lays a single egg on top of a paralysed caterpillar, which the larva then eats. This sand wasp has a pointed snout and a bulb-shaped tip on its abdomen.

15

WASPS

Oak marble gall-wasp ▽

Length: 4mm

This gall-wasp has a small reddish-brown body and grey wings. It lays its egg in a leaf bud, and as the larva feeds, the tree forms a solid lump around it.

Place	Date

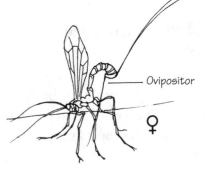

Ovipositor

♀

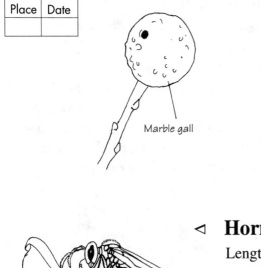

Marble gall

Ichneumon wasp △

Place	Date

Length: 22-30mm

This large, long-legged wasp has an extension, called an "ovipositor", which is longer than its body. It uses this to pierce holes in pine trees and to lay its eggs inside the tree.

◁ Hornet

Length: 22-30mm

The hornet is very large and has brown and yellow markings on its abdomen. It is less likely to sting than the common wasp.

Place	Date

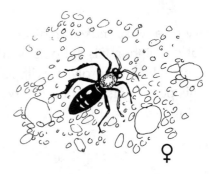

♀

German wasp ▷

Length: 15-20mm

This wasp has yellow and black markings along its abdomen. Along with the common wasp, it is Britain's commonest species.

Place	Date

Velvet ant △

Place	Date

Length: 15mm

Although its female has no wings, the velvet ant is actually a wasp. The female has a red rounded thorax, and a black abdomen marked with four light flecks and a light ring. The velvet ant can give you a nasty sting.

WASPS, SAWFLY, ANTS

Blue horntail

Place	Date

Length: 20-25mm

The head, thorax and first two segments of the male's abdomen are deep metallic blue. The female is blue all over. The blue horntail can be found in pine forests.

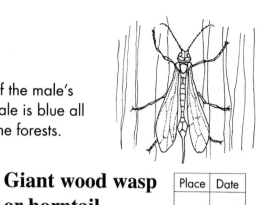

◁ ## Giant wood wasp or horntail

Place	Date

Length: 25-32mm

The giant wood wasp, or horntail, is large, black and hairy, with yellow stripes on its abdomen and a yellow pad behind its eye. Its larvae feed on wood for up to three years.

Birch sawfly

Place	Date

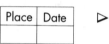

Length: 20-23mm

The birch sawfly has a dark body with a small yellow fleck around the top of its abdomen. Its larva has six pairs of extra "prolegs", as well as three pairs of true legs. It feeds on birch leaves in late summer.

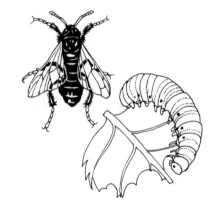

◁ ## Carpenter ant

Place	Date

Length: 8-18mm

The carpenter ant's thorax is reddish-brown, while its head and lower body are much darker. It nests in pine tree trunks, hollowing them out and often making the whole tree fall down. It is found in Europe and the USA.

Black ant

Place	Date

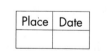

Length: 3-9mm

This ant is black, and common in gardens. The males die after mating, and the queens then start new nests or colonies on their own.

TRUE FLIES

◁ **Grey flesh fly**

Place	Date

Length: 6-17mm

The grey flesh fly has grey and black markings on its body, and reddish-brown eyes. It is common, and lays its eggs in carrion (dead rotting meat).

Hover fly ▷

Place	Date

Length: 10-14mm

This hover fly is brown, with three light stripes on each side of its abdomen. Hover flies can hover in the air as if they were not moving.

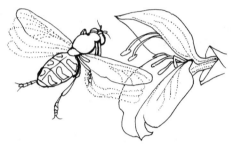

Greenbottle fly ▽

Place	Date

Length: 7-11mm

This fly is bottle green and can be found among flowers. Most species of greenbottle fly lay their eggs in carrion (dead rotting meat).

Place	Date

Horse fly △

Length: 20-25mm

A loud hum warns you that the female horse fly is about to bite you. The horse fly has a dark brown body, with light brown edges on each segment of its abdomen, and large green eyes.

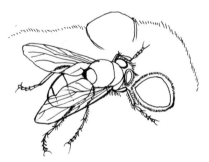

◁ **Dung fly**

Length: 10-12mm

You can find the dung fly around fresh cowpats, where the female lays her eggs. This one has a bright golden-coloured body. When dung flies are disturbed, they rise in a buzzing mass, but soon settle again.

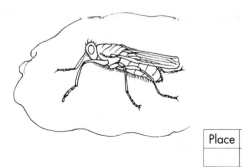

Place	Date

TRUE FLIES, ANT-LION

Bee fly ▷

Length: 10-11mm

Place	Date

The bee fly has a round furry body, and flies around garden flowers looking for nectar in early spring. It is most common in southern England.

Place	Date

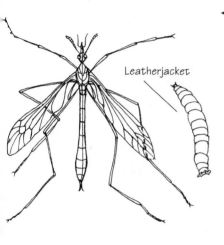

Leatherjacket

◁ Giant cranefly or daddy-long-legs

Length: 30-40mm

This large fly has a long spindly body and very long legs. It is often found near water. Its larvae are called "leatherjackets", and they eat root crops and grass roots.

Place	Date

Common gnat △ or mosquito

Length: 6-7mm

This common gnat is small, with a golden-brown body and very long thin legs. The female sucks blood from people and animals.

Black and yellow cranefly ▷

Length: 18-20mm

This cranefly has a long body, with black and yellow markings, and very long thin legs. In the summer, it can often be seen joined end to end with another cranefly while mating.

Place	Date

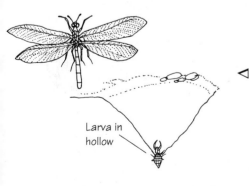

Larva in hollow

◁ Ant-lion

Place	Date

Length: 35mm

The ant-lion is long, with four broad white wings. Its larva traps ants and other insects in a sandy hollow and then sucks them dry. The ant-lion is not found in Britain and is rare in Europe except in the Mediterranean.

SCORPION FLY, LACY-WINGED INSECTS

Lacewings, snake flies and alder flies all have wings with fine, delicately patterned veins.

Scorpion fly ▽

Place	Date

Length: 18-22mm

The scorpion fly is so-called because of the male's tail, which curls up like a scorpion's. The male has a long yellow body with black markings, and a long "beak".

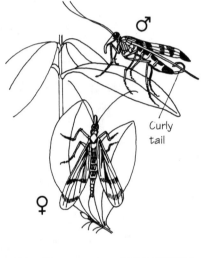

Curly tail

♂

♀

Giant lacewing ▽

Place	Date

Length: 15mm

You are most likely to spot the giant lacewing by night. It has large see-through wings covered in brown lace-like veins, and very long wavy antennae.

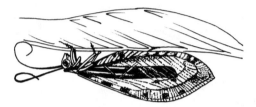

Place	Date

▽ Green lacewing

Length: 15mm

The green lacewing has four wings covered with green lace-like veins. You can find it mainly around gardens and hedges. Green lacewings often come into houses to hibernate through the winter.

Snake fly ▽

Place	Date

Length: 15-20mm

The snake fly is so-called because when it bends its head and thorax it looks like a cobra. This one has a long head and thorax and thin transparent wings.

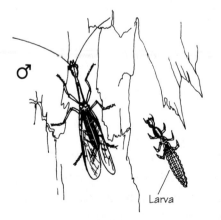

♂

Larva

Alder fly ▷

Length: 20mm

The alder fly lays its eggs in mats on the stems of water plants. It flies in a slow, heavy way. This alder fly has large brownish wings and long antennae.

Place	Date

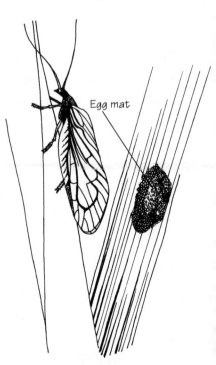

Egg mat

MAYFLY, STONEFLY, CRICKETS

Mayfly ▷

Length: 40mm

Place	Date

The adult mayfly does not live for long - sometimes for as little as a few hours. Its nymphs live in ponds and streams. This mayfly is large, with long tails and transparent brown striped wings.

Stonefly

Length: 22 mm

Place	Date

▽

The stonefly has long overlapping wings. Its nymphs have long tails and live on the river bottom, feeding on other small animals.

◁
◁

House cricket

Length: 16mm

Place	Date

You might hear the shrill song of the house cricket in and around greenhouses, heated buildings and rubbish heaps. It has a light brown body with dark markings, broad spiny back legs and short tails.

Field cricket ▷

Length: 20mm

Place	Date

The field cricket is extremely rare. It has a black body and legs, long antennae and brown wing cases. The male "sings" to attract a female by rubbing its wing cases together.

◁ ## Mole cricket

Length: 38-42mm

Place	Date

The outside of the mole cricket's thorax has grown forwards over its head, looking like an armour case. It has front feet shaped like spades, which it uses for digging. The male has a long whirring call. This cricket is almost extinct.

BUSH CRICKETS, GRASSHOPPER, STICK INSECT

Place	Date

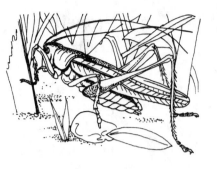

◁ **Great green bush cricket**

Length: 45-47mm

The great green bush cricket has long wings and antennae, and long thin back legs. It makes a loud shrill noise, moves slowly and never flies very far.

Wart-biter

 ▷

Length: 34-35mm

This extremely rare insect looks like the great green bush cricket, but it is smaller, with shorter antennae and dark markings on its green wings. It may bite when it is handled. People in Sweden used to use this insect to bite their warts.

Place	Date

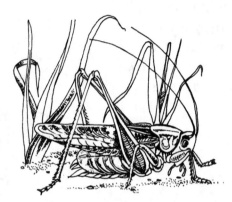

◁ **Large marsh grasshopper**

Length: 27-32mm

The rare grasshopper has a yellow and black abdomen and a red and brown head and thorax, with short antennae and long back legs. The male has a slow ticking song, and when it flies its wings look silvery.

Place	Date

Stick insect ▷

Length: up to 90mm

The stick insect is so-called because its very long thin green body looks like a stick with thin legs attached. There are no natural species in Britain, but some are kept as pets and have escaped into the wild.

Place	Date

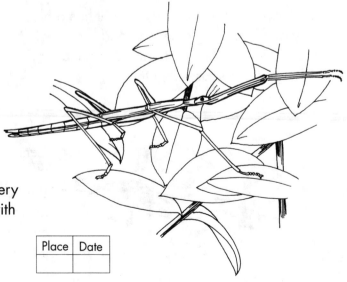

PRAYING MANTIS, COCKROACHES, EARWIG

Praying mantis ▷

Place	Date

Length: 60-80mm

The praying mantis has a long green body, with a small head and large front legs. It holds these together as if it is praying while it waits for its insect prey to come near. The praying mantis is not found in Britain.

◁ Common cockroach

Place	Date

Length: 25mm

The common cockroach is large, black and rounded, with spiny legs and long antennae. Its head is covered by the outside of the thorax, which has grown forwards, looking like a helmet. It eats waste in houses and other buildings. It does not fly.

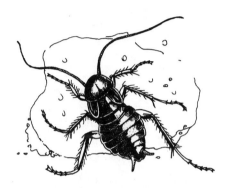

German cockroach ▽

Length: 13mm

The German cockroach has a light brown body, with two dark streaks on its head, and long folded wing cases. In spite of its name, it probably comes from North Africa or the Middle East.

Place	Date

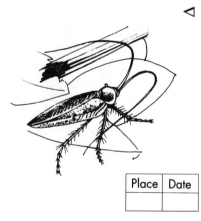

Place	Date

◁ Dusky cockroach

Length: 7-10mm

This cockroach is smaller than other cockroaches and, unlike them, it lives outside. It looks very like the German cockroach but, as its name suggests, is darker in colour.

Common earwig ▷

Length: 15mm

The common earwig is brown and has tiny wing cases and a long abdomen with pincers at the end. It spreads these and lifts them above its body when it feels threatened. The common earwig scavenges on small insects, fruits and leaves.

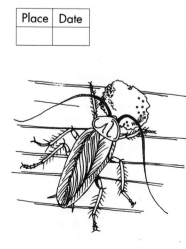

Place	Date

CHECKLIST

1 Devil's coach horse or cocktail beetle
2 Purple hairstreak
3 Great green bush cricket
4 Birch sawfly
5 Potter wasp
6 Great diving beetle
7 Sand wasp
8 Eyed hawk-moth
9 Green shieldbug
10 Horned dung beetle or minotaur beetle
11 Forester
12 Common cockroach
13 Silver Y
14 Praying mantis
15 Black bean aphid or blackfly
16 Marbled white
17 Vapourer
18 Blue horntail
19 Brimstone
20 Oak marble gall-wasp
21 Oak eggar
22 Wall brown
23 Common gnat or mosquito
24 Peach blossom
25 Giant cranefly or daddy-long-legs
26 Click beetle or skip-jack
27 Stonefly
28 Grey flesh fly
29 Puss moth
30 Ghost moth
31 Demoiselle agrion or beautiful demoiselle
32 Rove beetle
33 Green leafhopper
34 Common earwig
35 German wasp

36 Dung fly
37 Carpenter ant
38 Wasp beetle
39 Seven-spot ladybird
40 Large tortoiseshell
41 Musk beetle
42 German cockroach
43 Hummingbird hawk-moth
44 Great silver water beetle
45 Water cricket
46 Water beetle
47 Ruddy darter or ruddy sympetrum
48 Rose chafer
49 Death watch beetle
50 Six-spot burnet
51 Black and red froghopper
52 Clifden nonpareil or blue underwing
53 Peacock
54 Velvet ant
55 Wood tiger
56 Water scorpion
57 Wart-biter
58 Clouded yellow
59 Cardinal beetle
60 Giant lacewing
61 Death's head hawk-moth
62 Green lacewing
63 Red-tailed bumblebee
64 Brown argus
65 Bloody-nosed beetle
66 Bee fly
67 Scorpion fly
68 Leaf-cutter bee
69 Glow-worm
70 Nut weevil
71 Giant wood wasp or horntail
72 Lappet
73 Mayfly
74 Emperor moth

75 Cockchafer or maybug
76 Pond skater
77 Stick insect
78 Dusky cockroach
79 Large marsh grasshopper
80 Broad-bodied chaser or broad-bodied libellula
81 Hover fly
82 Red underwing
83 Horse fly
84 Black and yellow cranefly
85 Red and black burying beetle
86 Small white
87 Snake fly
88 Saucer bug
89 Water boatman or backswimmer
90 Greenbottle fly
91 Downy emerald
92 Banded agrion or banded demoiselle
93 Common ischnura or blue-tailed damselfly
94 Ruby-tailed wasp
95 Alder fly
96 Rose aphid or greenfly
97 House cricket
98 Lobster moth
99 Field cricket
100 Hornet
101 Cinnabar
102 Mole cricket
103 Garden tiger
104 Ichneumon wasp
105 Colorado beetle
106 Pearl-bordered fritillary
107 Black ant
108 Ant-lion
109 Stag beetle
110 Green tortoise beetle
111 Swallow-tailed moth

ISBN 0-439-44414-4

12 11 10 9 8 7 6 5 4 3 2 1   2 3 4 5 6 7/0

Printed in the U.S.A.   40
First Scholastic printing, October 2002